Prime Ministers of Canada

The Trudeau Era

By Douglas Baldwin and Patricia Baldwin

Weigl

CALGARY

www.weigl.com

Published by Weigl Educational Publishers Limited
6325 10 Street SE
Calgary, Alberta, Canada
T2H 2Z9

Website: www.weigl.com

Library and Archives Canada Cataloguing in Publication

Baldwin, Douglas, 1944-
       Trudeau era / Doug Baldwin.
(Prime ministers of Canada)
Includes index.
ISBN 1-55388-254-7 (bound).--ISBN 1-55388-255-5 (pbk.)

       1. Prime ministers--Canada--Biography--Textbooks.
2. Canada--History--1963- --Textbooks. I. Title. II. Series:
Prime ministers of Canada (Calgary, Alta.)
FC26.P7B342 2006   971.064'40922   C2006-902481-2

Printed in Canada
1 2 3 4 5 6 7 8 9 0 10 09 08 07 06

Cover: Pierre Trudeau is considered by some people to have been Canada's most captivating and charismatic prime minister.

Photo Credits: Canadian Press: pages 8, 9; **Glenbow Museum Archives:** page 5 (nc-6-11899); **Library and Archives Canada:** pages 4 (C-005327, C-010460, PA-033933, C-001971), 5 (C-00687, PA-128175), 20 9PA-140705), 37 (PA-128175); **Courtesy of Heather Hudak:** page 28; **Saskatchewan Archives:** page 4 (R-D700).

Every reasonable effort has been made to trace ownership and to obtain permission to reprint copyright material. The publishers would be pleased to have any errors or omissions brought to their attention so that they may be corrected in subsequent printings.

We acknowledge the financial support of the Government of Canada through the Book Publishing Industry Development Program (BPIDP) for our publishing activities.

Project Coordinator
Tatiana Tomljanovic

Design
Terry Paulhus

All of the Internet URLs given in the book were valid at the time of publication. However, due to the dynamic nature of the Internet, some addresses may have changed, or sites may have ceased to exist since publication. While the author and publisher regret any inconvenience this may cause readers, no responsibility for any such changes can be accepted by either the author or the publisher.

Contents

Canada's Prime Ministers

Since **Confederation**, there have been 22 Canadian prime ministers. Canada's prime ministers have come from many provinces and cultures. Some of them, such as the first prime minister, John A. Macdonald, were born in other countries. They came to Canada because they, or their parents, decided Canada was the best place to live and raise a family.

Canada's prime ministers are people of many talents and different interests. Some trained as lawyers, while others were journalists, doctors, farmers, writers, teachers, business people, and members of the **civil service**. Some of them fought as soldiers to protect Canada and her allies. All of them had one thing in common. They wanted to make Canada one of the best places in the world to live.

THE NEW NATION (CONFEDERATION TO 1896)

John A. Macdonald
(July 1, 1867–November 5, 1873; October 17, 1878–June 6, 1891)

Alexander Mackenzie
(November 7, 1873–October 8, 1878)

John J. C. Abbott
(June 16, 1891–November 24, 1892)

John S. D. Thompson
(December 5, 1892–December 12, 1894)

Mackenzie Bowell
(December 21, 1894–April 27, 1896)

Charles H. Tupper
(May 1, 1896–July 8, 1896)

TURN OF THE 20TH CENTURY (1896–1920)

Wilfrid Laurier
(July 11, 1896–October 6, 1911)

Robert L. Borden
(October 10, 1911–July 10, 1920)

TIME OF TURMOIL (1920–1948)

Arthur Meighen
(July 10, 1920–December 29, 1921; June 29, 1926–September 25, 1926)

Richard B. Bennett
(August 7, 1930–October 23, 1935)

William Lyon Mackenzie King
(December 29, 1921–June 28, 1926; September 25, 1926–August 7, 1930; October 23, 1935–November 15, 1948)

TIME OF TRANSITION (1948–1968)

TRUDEAU ERA (1968–1984)

Louis S. Saint Laurent
(November 15, 1948–June 21, 1957)

Pierre Elliott Trudeau
(April 20, 1968–June 3, 1979; March 3, 1980–June 30, 1984)

John George Diefenbaker
(June 21, 1957–April 22, 1963)

Charles Joseph Clark
(June 4, 1979–March 2, 1980)

Lester B. Pearson
(April 22, 1963–April 20, 1968)

John N. Turner
(June 30, 1984–September 17, 1984)

CONTEMPORARY CANADA (1984 TO PRESENT)

Martin Brian Mulroney
(September 17, 1984–June 13, 1993)

Jean J. Chrétien
(October 25, 1993–December 12, 2003)

Kim Campbell
(June 13, 1993–October 25, 1993)

Paul E. P. Martin
(December 12, 2003–February 6, 2006)

Stephen J. Harper
(February 6, 2006–)

Pierre Elliott Trudeau: Canada's Charismatic Leader

Pierre Elliott Trudeau placed third in a vote to decide "The Greatest Canadian" conducted by the CBC in November 2004. Canadians from coast to coast voted for whom in Canada's history they thought best embodied what being a Canadian is.

Pierre Elliott Trudeau shattered images. He enjoyed driving sports cars. He dated movie stars. He wore sandals and a buckskin jacket to work. Occasionally, he muttered obscenities. He made a pirouette behind the back of Queen Elizabeth II. Trudeau had charisma.

Trudeau did not mind controversy. He was determined to have his way when it really mattered. When he died in 2000, Trudeau was one of the most admired and most disliked of all Canadian prime ministers.

Trudeau was elected prime minister in 1968. Four years later, his popularity had declined so much that he was only able to form a minority government. The Liberals returned with a majority government in 1974, but Trudeau lost the next election in 1979 to Joe Clark's Progressive **Conservative Party**. Less than a year later, Trudeau returned as prime minister. He won the 1980 election and retired from politics in 1984. John Turner became the next prime minister.

Trudeau was best known for adopting official **bilingualism**, **patriating** the **Constitution**, passing the Charter of Rights and Freedoms, and fighting **separatism** in Quebec. Trudeau challenged Canadians to fight for what they believed. "If we want to preserve Canada" he said, "we must be willing to fight—not with guns, but with all the power of our minds and passion in our hearts."

Pierre Trudeau's fashion was always a point of interest throughout his political career. He was known to wear buckskin coats, hats, and even capes.

Keeping Canada Together

"I speak of a Canada where men and women of Aboriginal ancestry, of French and British heritage, of the diverse cultures of the world, demonstrate the will to share this land in peace, in justice, and with mutual respect. I speak of a Canada which is proud of, and strengthened by, its essential bilingual destiny, a Canada whose people believe in sharing and in mutual support, and not in building regional barriers."
Trudeau, 1982

Trudeau's Early Years

> "The memory I have of him being a kind of fun guy, the life of the party, running things, and having all these friends. My father would be arguing politics in a loud voice."
>
> *Trudeau on his father, Charles-Émile*

Joseph Philippe Pierre Yves Elliott Trudeau was born in Montreal, Quebec, on October 18, 1919. Pierre's parents were a good example of opposites attracting. Trudeau's father, Charles-Émile was loud and outgoing. He was the son of a Quebec farmer. Trudeau's mother, Grace, was quiet and thoughtful. She came from Montreal's English elite.

Pierre Trudeau's parents were bilingual. Although they spoke French and English at home, they preferred speaking English. Both parents were Roman Catholic.

Charles-Émile Trudeau established an automobile club. He charged members a fee for cheaper gasoline, towing, and repairs. Later, Charles-Émile sold the business to Imperial Oil for $1 million. He also owned the Montreal Royals baseball team, several mines, and an amusement park.

Pierre Trudeau had an older sister, Suzette, who was born in 1918. His younger brother, Charles Elliott, was born in 1922. Another brother died as a baby.

As a boy, Trudeau was shy and sensitive. He took after his mother, but Trudeau quickly toughened up under his father's influence.

When Trudeau turned 12, his family moved into a new house in a wealthy neighbourhood. The family often travelled throughout Canada and Europe. Trudeau was barely 15 when his father died suddenly from pneumonia.

After graduating from Collège Jean-de-Brébeuf in 1940, Trudeau entered law school at the Université de Montréal. As a student, Trudeau was **conscripted** into the Canadian army. While studying, Trudeau served with the military. However, he never fought overseas.

Trudeau was against conscription of Quebeckers, whom he felt had been betrayed by the Mackenzie King government. In 1942, he supported an anti-conscription candidate in a local election. Trudeau was eventually expelled from the Officers' Training Corps as a result of his **political activism**.

Trudeau continued his studies, graduating law school in 1943. Immediately after, he enrolled

TRUDEAU'S FORMAL EDUCATION

- Jean de Brébeuf College, bachelor of arts degree, 1940
- Université de Montréal, bachelor of civil law degree, 1943
- Harvard University, master of arts degree in political economy, 1945
- École des sciences politiques, Paris, 1946–1947
- London School of Economics, 1947–1948

in a graduate economics program at Harvard University in Cambridge, Massachusetts. From 1946 to 1948, he studied political science in Paris and economics at the London School of Economics.

After his studies, Trudeau backpacked through Eastern Europe, the Middle East, and Asia from 1948 to 1949. He was in China when the **Communist** Party took control in 1949. At this time, Trudeau was interested in **Marxist** ideas. He had attended a conference in communist Moscow where he was briefly arrested for throwing a snowball at a statue of Stalin. He also subscribed to several **leftist** magazines. As a

result, during the 1950s, the United States **blacklisted** Trudeau and refused him entry into the country. Trudeau later appealed the ban, and it was removed.

Throughout the 1950s, Trudeau sought to overthrow Quebec Premier Maurice Duplessis. He supported Quebec asbestos workers who went on strike for better working conditions and pay. With other young intellectuals, Trudeau founded the journal *Cité Libre*. Trudeau's writing earned him a reputation as a supporter of free speech and democracy. In 1961, he began teaching law at the Université de Montréal.

When Pierre Trudeau travelled to the Middle East in the late 1940s, he adopted much of the traditional garb of the region.

DID YOU KNOW?

Trudeau enjoyed taking long, canoe trips in northern Quebec. He once remarked, "paddling a canoe is a source of enrichment and inner renewal." After his death, he was given the Bill Mason Award for outstanding contributions to canoeing heritage.

"Trudeaumania"

> **"For those of us who were there when Pierre Trudeau was prime minister it was the magic of the man that is etched and cherished in the mind's eye. We embraced his diamond-sharp intellect, his irreverence, and the style of his leadership and life."**
>
> *Toronto Star editorial, 1999*

In 1965, the **Liberal Party** was looking for prominent French Canadians to become members of **Parliament**. Prime Minister Lester Pearson invited Trudeau and two of his colleagues, Jean Marchand and Gérard Pelletier, to run for the party in that year's election. Called the "three wise men," Trudeau, Marchand, and Pelletier won their seats. Trudeau entered politics to provide a strong voice for Quebec in the **federal government**. He also wanted to halt the growth of separatism in Quebec and strengthen the powers of the federal government.

Ambitious and smart, Trudeau established a reputation as a defender of the federal government against Quebec's demands. Pearson appointed Trudeau as minister of justice in 1967. In this role, Trudeau gained national attention for reforming divorce laws and for liberalizing the laws on abortion, homosexuality, and public lotteries. It was at this time that Trudeau made the comment, "The state has no place in the bedrooms of the nation."

As a member of Parliament (MP), Trudeau's casual dress sometimes upset his more conservatively dressed colleagues. His long hair, sandals, and loosely tied ascot were all new to the **House of Commons**. When former Prime Minister John Diefenbaker protested, Trudeau replied that he believed "people are more interested in ideas than dress." After decades of conservative politicians, Trudeau, who wore ascots and capes and drove a convertible, was a rare exception.

When Prime Minister Pearson retired, Trudeau was persuaded to run for the Liberal leadership. At the April 1968 Liberal leadership convention, Trudeau was elected leader of the party. He immediately called an election.

The 1968 Liberal leadership convention was held in Ottawa at the Ottawa Civic Centre. Trudeau was not elected party leader, and with it prime minister, until the fourth ballot.

The 1968 election campaign was marked by "Trudeaumania." Trudeau was mobbed by throngs of young people. Teenage girls swooned and screamed at Trudeau's public appearances. A gang of autograph seekers chased him across the Parliament Hill grounds.

Trudeau brought youthfulness and a promise of change. He was 48 years old, unwed, and much younger than most politicians of the time. Most thought he was handsome, witty, intelligent, and an exciting speaker. Trudeau was bilingual and a forceful leader.

Trudeau had a strong sense of justice and a deep love for Canada. People were impressed by Trudeau's vision of what he termed "a just society." In this society, he said, the rights of all Canadians would be respected, and everyone would enjoy the good things of life. Trudeau promised a better world.

Voters were swept up in a fever of enthusiasm. The day before the election, Trudeau attended the annual St.-Jean-Baptiste Day parade in Quebec. A riot started when several Quebeckers threw rocks and bottles filled with acid and paint at the bandstand where Trudeau was seated. Defying his aides' pleas to take cover, Trudeau stayed in his seat. He faced the rioters without a change in expression or a sign of fear. More than 290 people were arrested, and the riot was broadcast on the evening news. The image of the young politician showing such courage impressed many Canadians and helped him win the election.

In 1969, Trudeau visited the Canadian National Exhibition. The CNE is the world's largest annual exhibition of agriculture, manufacturing, industry, commerce, and the arts. It is held in Toronto.

DID YOU KNOW?

While at university during World War II, Trudeau and a friend dressed up as Prussian officers. They roared off on motorcycles with pointed steel helmets on their heads, startling all those they met on the road.

Trudeau's Family

Margaret Sinclair was born in 1948. She married Pierre Elliott Trudeau at the age of 22.

Trudeau was a bachelor when he became prime minister. He dated many women. Some of them, such Barbra Streisand, Kim Cattrall, and Margot Kidder, were celebrities. On March 4, 1971, he announced that he had married Margaret Sinclair, the daughter of a Liberal **cabinet minister,** in a private ceremony.

When Margaret was asked about her role in the marriage to the most famous man in Canada, she answered, "I want to be more than a rose in my husband's lapel." Margaret worked as a sociologist. Twelve people attended the wedding ceremony. Margaret had told her relatives that they were gathering for a family portrait. Trudeau's aides thought the couple were taking a ski vacation. Nine months later, the couple had a son, Justin. Trudeau was the first prime minister since John A. Macdonald to have a child while in office. The Trudeaus had two more sons—Alexandre "Sacha" and Michel.

Margaret resented her husband's work-related absences and felt she was raising their three young sons by herself. In a few instances, Margaret made news headlines. The press caught her smoking pot inside the prime minister's residence, and she was criticized for not wearing a conventional floor-length dress to an official White House dinner. The marriage soon began to fall apart.

Suffering from stress and bouts of depression, Margaret separated from Pierre in 1977. She became a jet setter. She gave "tell-all" interviews to Canadian and American magazines and appeared in two movies.

The Trudeaus divorced in 1984. Pierre kept custody of their three sons. A short time later, Margaret re-married Ottawa real-estate developer Fried Kemper. They had two children. After her second marriage, Margaret disappeared from the public eye.

In 1990, at age 71, Trudeau had a daughter, Sarah, with lawyer Deborah Coyne.

Even after their divorce, Margaret and Pierre remained close. In November 1998, they supported each other when their youngest son, Michel, an avid outdoorsman, was killed in an avalanche in British Columbia. When Pierre died in 2000, Margaret was at his bedside.

"Pierre Elliott Trudeau. The very words convey so many things to so many people. Statesman, intellectual, professor, adversary, outdoorsman, lawyer, journalist, author, prime minister. But more than anything, to me, he was dad. And what a dad. He loved us with the passion and the devotion that encompassed his life."

Justin Trudeau speaking at his father's funeral, October 3, 2000

Margaret Trudeau gained international infamy after partying at one of New York's most popular nightclubs, called Studio 54.

Trudeau and the Rise of Separatism

> "The governments of Canada and Quebec have been told by groups of self-styled revolutionaries that they intend to murder in cold blood two innocent men unless their demands are met. The kidnappers claim they act as they do in order to draw attention to instances of social injustice."
>
> *Trudeau's War Measures Act speech, October 16, 1970*

When Quebec Premier Maurice Duplessis died in 1959, the people of the province were ready for a change. During the 1960 election, John Lesage and the Liberal Party gained power in the province. Soon the "**Quiet Revolution**" began.

The Quiet Revolution had many goals. Many **francophones** wanted to be "masters in their own house." They felt like second-class citizens and wanted control over their own affairs. English

Pierre Trudeau's unmitigated desire for a strong federal government put him at odds with many Quebeckers, who wanted more power for their provincial government.

was the language of business, and the largest companies were owned by English-speaking Canadians or Americans. Francophones made less money than many citizens and higher-paying jobs in the province usually went to **anglophones**. People who spoke English were more likely to be promoted. The vast majority of immigrants to Quebec learned English, not French.

Lesage ensured the province's education system was modernized. The government also provided more hospitals and better health care services. Lesage passed laws to protect the French language and to ensure the survival of French-Canadian culture. Other laws guaranteed the rights of labour unions and provided social benefits. In 1969, the Quebec government took over the hydro-electric companies in the province as well.

Although Lesage and the Liberals were defeated in 1966, most French Canadians agreed with the goals of the Quiet Revolution. Some had different ideas about modernization. One group, which included Pierre Trudeau and Jean Chrétien, wanted Quebec to have more influence in the federal government in Ottawa. Others felt that Quebec should have fewer ties to the rest of Canada. They believed Quebec's culture and interests were separate from those of other Canadians. A smaller group of French Canadians wanted to "free" Quebec by creating a violent revolution. One such group was the Front de Libération du Québec (FLQ).

The FLQ was organized into cells, or small groups of people. Communication between cells was by secret code. Members of one cell did not know who was in another cell. Therefore, if one cell was discovered by the authorities, members could not release the names of members of other cells.

The Quiet Revolution turned bloody in April 1963. **Molotov cocktails** and dynamite rocked Montreal. In February 1969, bombs ripped

Jean Lesage was premier of Quebec from July 1960 to August 1966. He is sometimes called the father of the Quiet Revolution.

through the Montreal Stock Exchange, injuring 27 people. Between 1963 and 1970, the FLQ was responsible for more than 200 bombings.

On the morning of October 5, 1970, four FLQ members kidnapped British diplomat James Cross from his Montreal home. They demanded $500,000, plus television and radio time to broadcast FLQ beliefs to the Quebec people. They also asked for safe passage to Cuba or Algeria for themselves and 23 imprisoned FLQ members. Five days later, Pierre Laporte, the Quebec minister of labour, was also kidnapped.

The October Crisis

> "Well, there's a lot of bleeding hearts around who just don't like to see people with helmets and guns. All I can say is go on and bleed. It's more important to keep law and order in this society than to be worried about weak-kneed people who don't like the looks of helmets."
>
> *Trudeau on the use of the military during the FLQ crisis*

Quebec police were unable to locate the FLQ kidnappers, and people feared that the FLQ would strike again. Quebec Premier Robert Bourassa asked Trudeau for help, triggering the October Crisis. During this time, Trudeau asked Parliament to proclaim the War Measures Act. The War Measures Act allowed the government to temporarily suspend the Canadian Bill of Rights. Police could arrest, search, and question suspects without cause. The act was designed for emergency use when Canada was at war. It had never been used during peace. Trudeau declared separatist organizations and membership in them as illegal.

"I can assure you that the Government is most reluctant to seek such powers, and did so only when it became crystal clear that the situation could not be controlled unless some extraordinary assistance was made available on an urgent basis," said Trudeau.

In October 1970, tanks roamed the streets of Montreal, and soldiers in full battle gear raided homes in their hunt for the "terrorists." Montreal was put under a curfew, and almost 500 people were arrested and held without the right to a phone call. Most of these people had committed no crime other than appearing sympathetic to Quebec independence. Most Canadians did not question Trudeau's decision to invoke the War Measures Act. Polls

The events of the October Crisis landed 1,000 Canadian troops into Montreal, including the 3rd Batallion, Royal 22nd Regiment.

taken at the time showed that 88 percent of Canadians, including 85 percent of Quebeckers, supported Trudeau's decision. Trudeau's popularity soared as a result of his swift actions. However, some people questioned his decision to use such drastic means to resolve a crisis. Controversy over Trudeau's use of the War Measures Act continues today.

On October 17, 1970, police found Pierre Laporte's body in the trunk of an abandoned car. On November 6, one of Laporte's kidnappers was found hiding in a Montreal apartment closet. Other cell members were arrested on December 28 in an abandoned farmhouse 30 kilometres southeast of Montreal.

Ten years later, an official government inquiry revealed that Laporte's death had probably been accidental. One of the kidnappers likely grabbed the back of Laporte's shirt in an attempt to keep him quiet and inadvertently also grabbed Laporte's gold necklace strangling him to death.

Routine police investigation led to the discovery of James Cross. On December 3, 1970, police and soldiers surrounded the house where Cross was being held. He had been there for nearly nine weeks. Canadians watched as his release was negotiated. The kidnappers demanded safe passage to Cuba. Television crews in helicopters followed the kidnappers' car as it raced through downtown Montreal. Cross was released into the custody of the Cuban Consul. The kidnappers were flown to Cuba.

The FLQ was left in ruins. Separatists were firmly convinced that separatism for Quebec would have to be achieved through peaceful means, and Trudeau resolved to weaken separatist sentiments.

British Trade Commissioner James Cross was kidnapped while entering a taxi outside his Montreal home on the morning of October 5th, 1970.

FLQ AROUND THE WORLD AND BACK

On December 4, 1970, five FLQ members received passage to Cuba. They later moved to France. Eventually, they all returned to Canada and served short jail terms for kidnapping.

The Fight to Preserve Canada

"The Government of Quebec has made public its proposal to negotiate a new agreement with the rest of Canada… do you give the Government of Quebec the mandate to negotiate the proposed agreement between Quebec and Canada?"

Québécois were asked to vote "yes" or "no" during the 1980 referendum

The end of the FLQ crisis was not the end of separatism. Many Québécois, such as René Lévesque, still believed in achieving independence, but by lawful means.

Lévesque was a well-known journalist before becoming an influential minister in the Lesage government during the 1960s. Lévesque became frustrated with the slow movement of the Quiet Revolution. He resigned from the Liberal Party to found the Movement Souveraineté Association in 1967. The association joined forces with another separatist party in 1968 to form the **Parti Québécois** (PQ). Lévesque was elected party leader.

PQ support increased dramatically. The party promised to end corruption in Quebec politics, to protect the French language, and to provide aid for the less fortunate. To attract voters, the PQ announced that the question of separation would be decided in a referendum. In the 1976 election, Lévesque and the PQ won 69 of the 110 seats.

In 1979, the Parti Québécois announced it would hold a referendum on May 20, 1980. Quebeckers would vote on whether or not Quebec should separate from Canada.

Quebeckers were asked to vote "yes" or "no" with regard to whether they wished to give the Quebec government the right to negotiate provincial sovereignty.

Meanwhile, Trudeau and the Liberal Party had lost the 1979 election to Joe Clark's Progressive Conservative Party. Trudeau resigned as leader of the Liberal Party. However, soon after taking office, Clark was defeated in the House of Commons, and an election was called. Trudeau was persuaded to

The conflicting views of Pierre Trudeau and René Lévesque attracted the attention of U.S. magazines, including *Time*.

return as Liberal leader. Three months after his "retirement," Trudeau was elected prime minister. Ten weeks later, he led the federal anti-separation forces in the 1980 Quebec referendum.

Both sides bombarded Quebec with rallies, speeches, pamphlets, and radio and television ads. Lévesque and his followers claimed that a "yes" vote would protect French language and culture. Trudeau used his popularity to persuade Quebeckers to remain in Canada.

Canadians waited in suspense as the results trickled in. Almost 60 percent of the province voted to remain in Canada. The defeat of the Parti Québécois in the referendum was a milestone in Trudeau's crusade against Quebec separatism. In the wake of that victory, Trudeau pushed for a new Canadian constitution.

Trudeau was the face of the federalists for the 1980 Quebec referendum.

A New Constitution

> "I believe a constitution can permit the co-existence of several cultures and ethnic groups with a single state."
>
> *Trudeau, 1965*

Energized by the 1980 referendum results, Trudeau began working to achieve his most ambitious goals. First, he wanted to patriate Canada's Constitution. The **British North America (BNA) Act** was a British law, and only the British government could amend the act. Trudeau thought that Canada should control its own Constitution. He felt that the **premiers** and the federal government had to develop a formula to change or amend the Constitution. Trudeau also wanted to include a Charter of Canadian Rights and Freedoms in the Constitution. He wanted to ensure that every citizen's individual rights were protected.

Queen Elizabeth signed the Constitution Act during an outdoor ceremony on Parliament Hill.

Great Britain had always been willing to relinquish control over the BNA Act. The act had not been patriated because Ottawa and the provincial governments could not agree on an amendment method. Each province had its own demands. Quebec wanted veto power over all constitutional changes. It wanted to be able to protect French Canadian culture, language, and traditions. Alberta, Newfoundland, and British Columbia wanted complete control over their natural resources. Prince Edward Island wanted a guarantee that its needs would not be overlooked. Diverse groups, such as Aboriginal Peoples, women, and the Northwest Territories, wanted their rights protected and increased.

Most people supported changes to Canada's Constitution, but getting all of the provincial leaders to agree on the same changes was almost impossible. The next 18 months were filled with federal provincial negotiations. Only Ontario and New Brunswick were in favour of Trudeau's plan. The other provinces, called the "Gang of Eight," believed that Trudeau's plan would weaken provincial powers.

Finally, Trudeau threatened to take control. He said he would go to Great Britain alone and patriate the Constitution on his own terms. Following a **Supreme Court** decision, Trudeau agreed to meet with the premiers one more time. At a November 1981 conference, Trudeau sweetened the deal by adding a section that gives provinces the right to pass laws that override certain charter rights. Every premier but Quebec's René Lévesque agreed.

In a ceremony on Parliament Hill, the Queen signed Canada's new Constitution Act on April 17, 1982. Thirty thousand people gathered in Ottawa to watch the signing ceremony. In Quebec, however, flags were lowered to half-mast, and 25,000 people marched in protest in Montreal.

The signing ceremony was a crowning moment for Trudeau. He had fulfilled one of his lifelong goals. The newly declared Constitution included both an amending formula and a Charter of Rights and Freedoms. The objective of the Charter of Rights was to protect the rights of citizens and minorities. The charter guaranteed fundamental, democratic, mobility, legal, equality, and linguistic rights. Section 35 clarified issues of Aboriginal rights. It also established the Aboriginal rights of the **Métis**. Section 15, on equality rights, has been used to remedy discrimination against minority groups.

Trudeau's dream of a new constitution had been achieved, but at a price. He had tried to satisfy the needs of Quebec, but he only succeeded in satisfying the wishes of the other Canadian provinces. Quebec Premier Lévesque claimed that the new constitution had been imposed on Quebec against its will. Some Quebeckers felt betrayed. The Canadian Constitution, rather than providing a binding tie, further divided Quebec from the rest of the country.

CHARTER OF RIGHTS AND FREEDOMS

The Charter of rights and freedoms guarantees the rights and freedoms of all Canadians. All Canadian laws must follow the terms of the charter and allow freedom of speech, of thought, and of expression. However, the charter places "reasonable limits" on the rights and freedoms Canadians enjoy.

Section 33 gives Canadian provinces the right to pass laws that ignore or override certain charter rights. Section 33 was added to give Canadian provinces flexibility when dealing with their respective citizens. Quebec has used this clause to maintain its language laws.

Trudeau and Minority Rights

"My father said: 'Justin, never attack the individual. We can be in total disagreement with someone without **denigrating** them.' "

Justin Trudeau

Pierre Trudeau sought to establish a just society for groups that had been traditionally excluded. Under Trudeau, Canada overhauled its immigration policies. For the first time, Canada looked beyond Europe for a source of immigrants. Canada received its fair share of refugees between the 1960s and the 1980s, including those from Czechoslovakia, Tibet, Uganda, Chile, and Vietnam.

Gradually, the source of immigration to Canada switched from Europe to Asia. In 1966, 87 percent of Canada's immigrants came from Europe. During the 1980s, only 27 percent of Canada's immigrants came from Europe, whereas 46 percent travelled from Asia, and 15 percent arrived from the Caribbean and South and Central America. Visible ethnic minorities became a large part of Canada's social fabric. In 1971, the federal government announced that Canada was a multicultural country within a bilingual framework and gave ethnic groups official status legally recognizing them as distinct. The face of Canada was rapidly changing.

In 1978, Canada established three categories of immigrants. The refugee category includes people who are forced to leave their country because of invasion, disaster, or persecution. To obtain immigrant status, these people are assessed on their ability to adapt to life in Canada. In the second category, Canadian relatives willing to support family members can sponsor their parents, spouses, grandparents

Immigrants have brought their culture to Canada. This includes music, festivals, and food.

under the age of 60, and unmarried children under the age of 19. All other immigrants are assessed on the "points" system. The points system assigns points to immigrants for education, experience, language, adaptability, and age.

In 1969, the Trudeau government announced its plans to scrap the 1876 Indian Act. The government's plans were spelled out in the June 1969 "White Paper." It called for the advancement of individual rights rather than the collective rights of Aboriginal Peoples. The White Paper intended to integrate Aboriginal Canadians into the rest of society rather than treat them as a separate group. Responsibility for services to Aboriginal Peoples would be transferred from the federal government to the provinces.

Aboriginal Peoples across the country opposed the government's plans. The resistance was led by the newly formed National Indian Brotherhood. Its leaders claimed that Aboriginal Canadians were interested in self-government, not assimilation, and the White Paper would lead to the destruction of the country's Aboriginal Peoples. Surprised by the reaction, the Trudeau government withdrew White Paper. The government did very little with this issue until a 1973 Supreme Court decision confirmed the legality of Aboriginal land claims. In response to the ruling, Ottawa established an Office of Native Claims to rule on Aboriginal land claims.

In a 1977 report, the commissioner of the Indian Claims Commission said, "It is clear that most Indian claims are not simple issues... they are the most visible part of the much, much more complex question of the relationship between the original inhabitants of this land and the powerful cultures which moved in upon them."

Economic Issues

> "He was highly intelligent and intellectual. He read all of his briefing documents, including the footnotes. He just wasn't interested in economics. He listened to everything and understood it. But, in the end, he had one priority: national unity."
>
> *Bernard Ostry, a well-known Canadian bureaucrat, on Trudeau's indifference to economic matters*

The Canadian economy began to slow down in the early 1970s. In 1973, the Organization of the Petroleum Exporting Countries (OPEC) reduced the world supply of oil. The price of oil increased dramatically. Subsequent increases in the cost of food, housing, and other consumer goods led to a frightening jump in the cost of living. Inflation reached critical proportions. By the mid-1970s, Trudeau faced high inflation and unemployment rates.

Economists and politicians searched for solutions. One of Trudeau's aides later wrote, "We tried a billion different ways to deal with inflation without necessarily putting millions of people out of work." The Bank of Canada warned that rising costs were undermining the country's ability to function efficiently and to compete internationally.

Despite opposing wage and price controls in the 1974 election campaign, Trudeau reversed his policy and introduced the Anti-Inflation Act in October 1975. This came only after failed attempts at getting employers and unions to voluntarily agree to wage restrictions.

The act limited increases in wages and prices. It applied to all federal employees and to private companies with 500 or more employees. Farmers and fishers, for example, were exempt from price controls. Increases in wages were capped at 10 percent in the first year, 8 percent in the second year, and 6 percent in the third year. The act was overseen by the Anti-

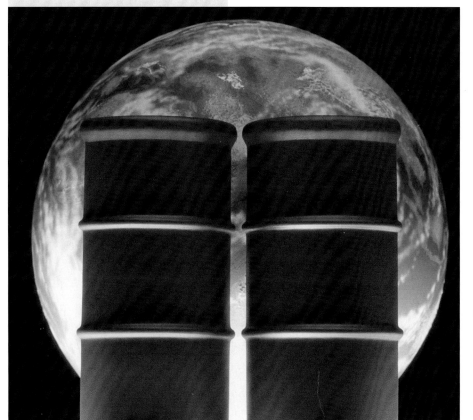

In 2004, OPEC countries continued to control a large majority of the world's crude oil reserves. Accounting for more than 895 barrels of oil, or 78 percent of the world's total reserves.

Inflation Board. The board investigated such things as gas prices, wages, insurance premiums, and food prices. About 4.2 million Canadians had their wage increases limited.

Many Canadians objected to wage controls. It limited their earning potential. Some workers had salary increases rolled back. Public sector workers, especially low-paid workers in schools, hospitals, and municipal governments, were affected the most. Unions were severely restricted in their ability to bargain for higher pay.

In 1976, the Canadian Labour Council, which represented the largest body of organized workers, called for a day of protest against wage controls. All workers, unionized and non-unionized, were asked to protest by not going to work on October 14. More than one

WAGE-PRICE SPIRAL

When businesses must buy more expensive goods to manufacture their products, they raise their prices. When the price of goods increases, workers demand higher wages. When employers are forced to pay higher wages, they raise their prices. This is what economists call a "wage-price spiral." The cycle seemed endless in the mid-1970s. As Canada's inflation rate increased, so did unemployment.

million workers walked off their jobs. This was the largest organized labour protest in North-American history.

Wage and price controls were phased out in 1978. The Anti-Inflation Board was dissolved the following year.

Inflation refers to a general rise in prices across the entire economy. It is not related to a product's price rising or falling due to supply and demand. It is more closely related to how much money is circulating in an economy.

A Canadian Energy Policy

In 1973, the Arab-Israeli war led to an increase in the cost of oil, as Arab countries drastically reduced oil exports to the United States. As a result, Alberta's oil became more valuable. Trudeau put a tax on Alberta's oil exports to help pay for oil in central and eastern Canada.

Canada's oil reserves had been under the control of U.S. corporations, and most of profits went to them. When oil prices quadrupled, few of the benefits went to Canadians. The **New Democratic Party** (NDP) first proposed the idea of creating a government-run oil company. Since the Liberals headed a **minority government** in which the NDP held the balance of power, Petro-Canada was created.

Petro-Canada became a symbol of Canadian **nationalism**. By 1980, Petro-Canada had become one of Canada's largest petroleum companies. Later, it led the way in finding large oil fields in the Grand Banks off the east coast of Newfoundland.

Petro-Canada refined crude oil, producing gasoline, diesel, jet fuel, heating oil, asphalt, and other products. Working closely with other companies, governments, and environmental organizations, Petro-Canada

In 2006, Petro-Canada employed more than 5,000 people around the world.

became an environmental leader. It removed lead from gasoline, reduced emissions of **greenhouse gases**, and developed cleaner-burning alternative fuels.

In 1979, the Iranian Revolution inflated world oil prices by 150 percent. When Trudeau refused to allow Canada's oil prices to rise to world prices, his relations with Alberta became strained. In October 1980, Trudeau introduced the National Energy Program (NEP). The federal government wanted more control over the country's energy. Trudeau declared that Alberta's oil profits must be shared throughout the country. Alberta's premier, Peter Lougheed, threatened to take the NEP to court.

The NEP had three main objectives. It sought to increase Canadian ownership in the oil industry, to make Canada self-sufficient in oil, and to make more money for the federal government. As part of the program, Ottawa kept the national oil price low.

Albertans believed that the NEP was designed to strip their province of its natural wealth. By keeping the oil prices below world market prices, the NEP was **subsidizing** the eastern provinces. Premier Lougheed reduced Alberta's oil production. A newspaper poll showed that more than 80 percent of Albertans supported the premier's actions. Lougheed announced on national television that oil shipments to the rest of Canada would be cut. As a result, the NEP was revised so that the price of Canadian oil would rise to the world price.

The justification for the NEP died when oil prices began to fall in the early 1980s. The program was dismantled when Brian Mulroney and the Conservative Party won the 1984 election. The NEP, however, left a legacy of Albertan anger toward Trudeau.

The National Energy Program was very unpopular in Alberta, where energy revenues are a main source of wealth for the province.

Issues with The United States: Economic Nationalism

> "Living next to you is like sleeping with an elephant; no matter how friendly and even-tempered is the beast, one is affected by every twitch and grunt."
>
> *Trudeau speaking to the American National Press Club, 1969*

In 1968, the United States created laws for **multinational** U.S. companies. U.S. plants in Canada were ordered to return more of their profits to the United States. U.S. companies also had to invest more money in the United States than in Canada and buy U.S. goods rather than Canadian goods. The U.S. government also told these multinational companies with which countries they could and could not trade. Canadian companies owned by Americans, for example, were not allowed to trade with the communist country of Cuba.

Trudeau set out to reduce Canada's economic dependence on the United States. In 1968, a Canadian government report recommended the creation of a special agency to deal with multinational companies. Two years later, another report suggested that Canadians have at least 51 percent ownership in multinational companies. The report also recommended that it be made illegal for companies operating in Canada to refuse legitimate export orders from any country, regardless of the nature of that country's relations with the United States. Finally, it proposed that any future takeovers of Canadian businesses by foreign-owned firms would require the approval of the Canadian government,

After being elected prime minister, Pierre Trudeau set out to reduce Canadian dependence on the United States.

and, in "key sectors" of the economy, no foreign takeovers should be allowed.

Many Canadians agreed that Canada should have greater control over its own economy. In 1974, Trudeau established the Foreign Investment Review Agency (FIRA) to review all proposals for foreign takeovers of existing businesses and examine the creation of new foreign-owned businesses in Canada. FIRA was designed to slow down U.S. control of Canadian industries and natural resources. It acted as a watchdog to ensure that any foreign takeovers of Canadian companies would be in Canada's best interests.

The United States viewed FIRA as an unfriendly action toward American business. In reality, FIRA approved nine out of ten applications for foreign takeovers. The National Energy Program and Petro-Canada also attempted to reduce dependence on the United States. The NEP was created to guarantee the security of Canada's oil and gas supplies and to provide Canadians with the opportunity to increase their ownership of the energy industry. Canadian control of the energy sector increased from 22 percent to 33 in the first two years of the NEP.

Herb Gray was a member of Trudeau's Cabinet. He chaired a committee that drew up recommendations about foreign investment in Canada. This report led to the creation of FIRA.

Issues with the United States: Foreign Policy

> "I will use all my strength to bring about a just society to a nation living in a tough world."
>
> *Trudeau, April 7, 1968*

The tensions that had plagued Canadian-American relations in the 1960s spilled over into the 1970s and 1980s. Trudeau and U.S. President Richard Nixon did not work well together. Later, Trudeau had little sympathy for the extreme anti-Soviet views of President Ronald Reagan.

Many Americans thought Trudeau was a **pacifist** and a leftist. Some considered him a communist. During a visit to the Soviet Union in 1971, Trudeau said the overwhelming American presence in Canada posed "a danger to our national identity from a cultural, economic and perhaps even military point of view."

During his visit to Ottawa in 1972, Nixon declared that the "special relationship" between Canada and the United States was over. "It is time for us to recognize," he stated, "that we have very

President Richard Nixon and Prime Minister Pierre Trudeau had trouble finding common ground on many issues.

separate identities; that we have significant differences; and that nobody's interests are furthered when these realities are obscured."

Despite the tensions between Canada and the United States, the Nixon government still tried to pressure Canada to participate in the supervision of the Vietnam War peace talks. The Americans were fighting on the side of South Vietnam and losing. In an attempt to force North Vietnam to negotiate peace, Nixon launched a major bombing offensive. Trudeau condemned the Nixon administration for prolonging the war and refused to help.

Trudeau also strongly disliked the U.S. Strategic Defense Initiative, known as "Star Wars." He believed that Star Wars would increase the arms race. Trudeau was worried by the United States' belief that the West could win a nuclear war. At a press conference in 1983, Trudeau expressed concern over U.S. policy in Central and South America. He complained that the United States supported Chile, El Salvador, and Guatemala, countries that abused human rights. Trudeau also openly condemned the United States for its attack on the tiny Caribbean island of Grenada.

Despite these problems, Canada maintained its commitments to the U.S.-led **North American Aerospace Defense Command** (NORAD) and remained a member of the **North Atlantic Treaty Organisation** (NATO). In addition, Trudeau attempted to maintain friendly relations with the United States by permitting them to test its **cruise missiles** over Canadian territory despite vocal protests of Canadian peace groups and Aboriginal Peoples.

Cruise missiles were tested in northern Canada during the 1980s under Prime Minister Trudeau's administration.

TESTING CRUISE MISSILES

In 1983, the Trudeau government allowed the United States to test the accuracy of cruise missiles, without war heads, in northern Alberta. Aboriginal Canadians objected. They argued that the testing broke treaty agreements. Greenpeace and other Canadian environmentalists protested the testing and appealed to the courts. The courts ruled against them, and the testing continued.

Canada and the World

Speaking to the United Nations in 1978, Pierre Trudeau outlined a four point "Strategy of Suffocation" aimed at stopping all nuclear weapon development. The strategy included a cutoff of all material capable of undergoing nuclear fission.

Trudeau's efforts in foreign affairs gained him worldwide respect. However, Trudeau rejected former Prime Minister Lester Pearson's belief that Canada should be an important player on the world stage. Trudeau thought that Canada was "a modest power." He believed that Canada should concentrate on its internal problems, such as the rise of separatism in Quebec, rather than trying to solve the world's problems.

Trudeau reduced Canada's armed forces. He cut the number of Canadian troops stationed in Europe and on peacekeeping duties. Near the

For his efforts to quell Cold War tensions and halt nuclear weapon development, such as the U.S. Navy nuclear tests at Bikini Atoll, Trudeau received the Albert Einstein Peace Prize in 1985.

end of his time as prime minister, Trudeau embarked on a peace mission to try to reduce nuclear tensions between the Soviet Union and the United States. Trudeau personally took his plan to Western capitals as well as to Moscow and Beijing. He met with little success. The Americans believed Trudeau should have consulted them in advance. Trudeau believed that if he had American approval, the Soviets would not trust him.

Trudeau was the only Western leader to make peace initiatives between the **Cold War** superpowers during the 1980s. Some viewed his peace mission as a failure. Trudeau, on the other hand, felt that the effort alone was of importance.

Trudeau's first major foreign policy shift came in 1970. Despite opposition from the U.S. government, Trudeau wanted to end China's isolation from the rest of the world. Most Western nations supported Taiwan as the legitimate government of China, but Canada

Fidel Castro became the leader of Cuba in 1959. Currently, he is the world's longest serving head of government.

recognized the communist People's Republic of China as the legitimate government. The following year, China and Canada established embassies in each other's country. This was the first time in more than 20 years that communist China had diplomatic relations in North America.

Trudeau established another friendly relationship with a communist country—Cuba. Although the United States had stopped all relations with Cuba in 1959, Trudeau once again set Canada on an independent course and paid an official visit to Cuba in January 1976. He was the first Canadian prime minister to do so.

Trudeau hugged communist leader Fidel Castro. He gave Cuba $4 million and loaned the country another $10 million. In Trudeau's speech before a crowd of 25,000 cheering Cubans, he declared "Long live Prime Minister and Commander-in-Chief Fidel Castro. Long live Cuban-Canadian friendship. Viva Cuba!"

Trudeau argued that Canada should keep its own independent foreign policy. Trudeau

and Castro developed a close, personal relationship and remained friends for years. Castro was among the world leaders at Trudeau's funeral. He declared that Trudeau was a "world-class statesman."

Trudeau also took a stand on human rights issues in other parts of the world. He strongly opposed **apartheid** in South Africa and in 1970, imposed an arms **embargo** on South Africa. In 1977, he stopped all trade assistance programs.

In October 1973, Pierre Trudeau became the first Canadian Prime Minister to make an official visit to China.

Language Issues

> "French Canada can survive not by turning in on itself but by reaching out to claim every aspect of Canadian life."
>
> *Trudeau speaking in favour of the Official Languages Act, 1986*

When Pierre Trudeau went into politics, he wanted to prevent Quebec separatism by making French Canadians feel at home across Canada.

In 1967, the Royal Commission on Bilingualism and Biculturalism warned that unless "an equal partnership" between French and English-speaking Canada was formed, the country was likely to break up. The commission stated that "Canada, without being fully conscious of the fact, is passing through the greatest crisis in its history."

The commission's report contained 100 recommendations and formed the basis of Trudeau's 1969 Official Languages Act. The report recommended that Canada be formally declared bilingual and that French and English be given equal status in the courts, in Parliament, and in government services. The Official Languages Act declared that French and English were the official languages of Canada. It also stated that all federal institutions had to provide their services in English and French. The act was supported by all federal parties. However, many English-speaking Canadians felt that there were not enough French-speaking people outside Quebec to justify the costs of bilingualism.

Despite mixed reactions, bilingualism was instated. With money from the federal government, the nine English-speaking provinces improved French language classes in schools. New Brunswick declared itself officially bilingual. In 1979, the Supreme Court restored French language rights in Manitoba. Companies now had to label their products in both languages across the country.

While the 1969 Official Languages Act did much to further language equality in Canada, constitutional limits leave such services as traffic signs under municipal jurisdiction, allowing cities to choose whether or not they offer traffic signs in both languages.

Trudeau's Legacy

> **"I speak of a Canada where men and women of aboriginal ancestry, of French and British heritage, of the diverse cultures of the world, demonstrate the will to share this land in peace, in justice, and with mutual respect."**
>
> *Trudeau, 1982*

On February 29, 1984, after a long walk in the snow, Trudeau announced his intention to retire. Four months later he left office, and his successor, John Turner, was sworn in as prime minister.

Trudeau returned to his Montreal law practice. He travelled extensively and spent time writing his memoirs. In his last years, Trudeau suffered from Parkinson's disease and prostate cancer. On September 28, 2000, just a few days before his 81st birthday, Pierre Elliott Trudeau died of pneumonia.

Canadians lined up in Ottawa for hours to pay their last respects to Trudeau, who lay in state on Parliament Hill. Across the country, flags flew at half-mast. Canadians watched the funeral on television, watching as Trudeau's eldest son, Justin, delivered a moving eulogy to his father. Justin and Sacha both wore red roses, their father's trademark.

At Trudeau's funeral on October 3, 2000, the country mourned, and leaders from around world, including Fidel Castro, came to pay their respects.

Trudeau was a charismatic figure who dominated Canadian politics. He aroused passionate reactions, especially in western Canada and Quebec. Some French Canadians thought he had "sold them out" to English-speaking Canada. Many Canadians felt that Trudeau's economic policies were weak. Inflation and unemployment remained high. Yet, during his time as prime minister, the United Nations reported that Canada had the world's best quality of life.

John Turner: Prime Minister for 80 Days

Under Turner, the Liberal Party lost the federal election to the Conservatives. It was the largest landslide victory in Canadian history for the Conservatives.

John Napier Turner was born in Richmond, Great Britain, on June 7, 1929. His father was a gunsmith, and his mother was a Canadian student working towards a Ph.D. at the London School of Economics. When Turner was three, his father died. His mother moved the family to her hometown in British Columbia and later to Ottawa because of a job opportunity.

Turner attended Ashbury College and St. Patrick's before his mother married a wealthy Vancouver businessman. The family moved west, and Turner enrolled at the University of British Columbia. He studied political science and economics. A brilliant student, as well as a talented track and field athlete, Turner graduated at the top of his class and earned a Rhodes Scholarship to study law at Oxford University in Great Britain. Turner later went to France to work on a Ph.D. at the University of Paris. Returning to Canada in 1953, he joined a law firm in Montreal. Eight years later, he was elected to the House of Commons. When Trudeau became prime minister, he appointed Turner minister of justice and later minister of finance. In 1976, after Trudeau did not support his plans to lower inflation, Turner resigned from politics and returned to his law firm.

When Trudeau resigned in 1984, Turner was elected Liberal Party leader. He was sworn in as prime minister on June 30. Turner had been out of office for several years, and his political skills were rusty. He called an election right away. However, the voters gave the Liberals 40 seats and the Conservatives 211 seats. Turner had been prime minister for only 80 days.

> **"I don't believe our future depends on our yielding those economic levers of sovereignty to become a junior partner in Fortress North America to the United States."**
>
> *Turner, October 12, 1988*

Turner slowly rebuilt the Liberal Party. He doubled the party's seats in the 1986 election, but Conservative Party leader Brian Mulroney won again.

Turner's most memorable moment as leader of the opposition came in the 1988 election campaign with his condemnation of the Free Trade Agreement. Despite his many years in business, Turner's vision of Canada went beyond making money. He understood the risks to Canadian business and economic independence involved in signing the Free Trade Agreement. He fought to persuade Canadians to defeat the Conservative Party, which supported the Free Trade Agreement. Unfortunately, his efforts failed to topple the Conservatives.

Turner resigned as leader in 1990 and returned to his law practice in Toronto. Jean Chrétien became the new Liberal Party leader.

Turner remains active in politics. In 2003, he attended the Liberal leadership convention and watched as Paul Martin was voted leader of the Liberal Party.

Joe Clark:
A Hardworking Prime Minister

Joe Clark held four different positions in the Cabinet of Prime Minister Brian Mulroney. Clark was Minister of National Defense, Minister of Justice, Minister of Constitutional Affairs and the Secretary of State for External Affairs.

Charles Joseph Clark was born on June 5, 1939, in High River, Alberta. His father was a newspaper owner and editor. Growing up, Joe delivered his father's *High River Times*. When he was in Grade 11, he won a public-speaking scholarship. The prize was a trip to Ottawa. Instead of visiting museums, Joe headed for the House of Commons, where he met future prime minister, John Diefenbaker.

Politics became Clark's passion. At the University of Alberta, where he studied history, English, and political science, Clark was active in student politics. He became student president of the Progressive Conservative Student Federation, and taught himself French.

After graduation, he worked for Diefenbaker's election campaign. Clark's political activities carried on. He served as president of the Progressive Conservative Student Federation and worked for Davie Fulton in the British Columbia election in 1963. Soon after, Clark worked for Peter Lougheed, the new provincial leader of the Conservatives in Alberta.

In 1972, Clark was elected to the House of Commons. The following year, he married Maureen McTeer. She was a prominent lawyer and champion of the rights of women and children. They had one daughter, Catherine.

Clark soon attracted attention as a dedicated and able young politician. In 1976, he became leader of the Progressive Conservative Party.

Similar to previous Conservative leaders, Clark found it difficult to compete with Trudeau's charismatic image. The press made fun of his awkward nature. "We will not take this nation by storm, by stealth or by surprise. We will win it by work," Clark declared shortly after being elected party leader. Clark's hard work brought the Conservative Party victory in the 1979 election. Clark formed a minority government.

At the age of 39, Charles Joseph Clark became Canada's youngest prime minister.

When Trudeau resigned as Liberal leader, Clark decided to privatize Petro-Canada. He announced plans to raise gasoline taxes. It would be, he stated, "short term pain for long term gain." Three days later, the opposition parties passed a vote of **non-confidence**, and an election was called. Clark lost the election to Pierre Trudeau. Trudeau's Liberal Party won a majority government.

Clark retired from politics in 1993. However, in 1998, he was re-elected leader of the Progressive Conservative Party and returned to the House of Commons. The Conservatives merged with the Alliance Party in 2003, and Clark again retired from politics.

Clark stated, "I think that there are times in public life when you have to put your party's interest and your country's interest first, and that's what I've tried to do."

Minority Government

As of 2006, there have been 12 minority governments in Canada. A minority government is created when no one political party has the majority of the seats in the House of Commons. To form the government, several parties, which control the majority of the seats, must work together.

Timeline

1910s	1920s	1930s	1940s

PRIME MINISTERS

Trudeau is born on October 18, 1919. 	Trudeau's younger brother, Charles Elliott Trudeau, is born on 1922. John Turner is born on June 7, 1929.	Joe Clark is born on June 5, 1939. 	Trudeau backpacks through Eastern Europe, the Middle East, and Asia from 1948–1949.

CANADA

The first Calgary Stampede is held on September 2, 1912. The Conscription Crisis takes place in 1917. The Winnipeg General Strike occurs in 1919.	Marijuana is made illegal in Canada in 1923. Banting and Best invent insulin in 1921. 	Cairine Wilson becomes Canada's first female Senator in 1930. The Canadian Broadcasting Corporation (CBC) is established in 1936. Canada declares war on Germany on, September 10, 1939.	Canada declares war on Italy on June 10, 1940. Canada joins the United Nations in 1945.

WORLD

World War I takes place from 1914–1918. 	The first full-length all-Technicolor motion picture, *The Toll of the Sea*, premiers in 1922.	Germany attacks Poland on September 1, 1939. Britain declares war on Germany on September 3, 1939.	Japan bombs Pearl Harbor on December 7, 1941. D-Day takes place on June 6, 1944.

EXTRA RACE RESULTS Los Angeles Times NIGHT Pictorial

IT'S WAR!

**Hostilities Declared by Japanese;
350 Reported Killed in Hawaii Raid**

U.S. Battleships Hit;   Air Bombs Rained
7 Die in Honolulu   on Pacific Bases

1950s   1960s   1970s

PRIME MINISTERS

Trudeau is blacklisted by the United States in 1950.

Trudeau becomes prime minister in 1968.

Trudeau passes the War Measures Act on October 16, 1970.

CANADA

Canada sends troops to Korea in 1950. The Massey Report on Canadian culture is released in 1951.

A maple leaf design becomes Canada's national flag in 1964. Canadians are issued social insurance cards for the first time in April 1964.

Front de Libération du Québec kidnaps British diplomat James Cross on October 5, 1970. The beaver becomes an official symbol of Canada on March 24, 1975.

WORLD

The Soviet Union launches Sputnik in 1957.

The Cuban missile crisis takes place in 1962.

Terrorists attack at the Olympic Games in Munich in 1972.

Did You Know?

In 1977, the Lévesque government made French the language of business and government in Quebec. All signs and billboards had to be written and displayed in French. Immigrant children would learn French in the school system, not English. Only children whose parents had been educated in English would be sent to English-language schools.

In 1965, John Turner was vacationing in Barbados when he saw a swimmer struggling in the rough surf. Turner, a competitive swimmer at university, swam out and rescued the man. Nineteen-year old John Turner had saved former prime minister, John Diefenbaker.

In 2004, Montreal-Dorval Airport was renamed Montreal-Pierre Elliott Trudeau International Airport in honour of the former prime minister. Its passenger traffic makes it the third-busiest airport in Canada.

On June 10, 2006, a mountain was dedicated to Pierre Trudeau. Mount Pierre Elliott Trudeau is located in the Rocky Mountains between Jasper, Alberta, and Prince George, British Columbia.

Following his tenure as prime minister, Joe Clark left politics and took teaching positions at the University of California and the American University in Washington, DC.

The Canadian Press named Pierre Trudeau "Newsmaker of the Year" a record 10 times and, in 1999, named him "Newsmaker of the 20th Century."

Test Your Knowledge

Question:

Which of the following prime ministers served the shortest amount of time in office?

A) Trudeau
B) Clark
C) Turner

C) Turner

Question:

Which province was most against Trudeau's energy policies?

A) Alberta
B) Newfoundland
C) Ontario

A) Alberta

Question:

Which of the following people were kidnapped by the FLQ?

A) Frank Ross
B) Charles Joseph Clark
C) Pierre Laporte

C) Pierre Laporte

Question:

Which prime minister was blacklisted by the U.S. government?

Trudeau

Question:

Did Joe Clark's Conservative Party have a minority government or a majority government while he was prime minister?

minority

Question:

Who did Trudeau marry while he was prime minister?

Margaret Sinclair

Question:

What is the name of the oil company Trudeau created?

Petro-Canada

Question:

What does FLQ stand for?

Front de Libération du Québec

Question:

What party did Turner belong to?

Liberal Party

Activity

On October 5, 1970, James Cross, the British Trade Commissioner, was kidnapped in Montreal by the FLQ. The FLQ ransom demands included the release of 23 political prisoners, $500,000 in gold, the broadcast and publication of the FLQ **Manifesto**, and an aircraft to take the kidnappers to Cuba or Algeria. Five days later, another cell of the FLQ kidnapped Pierre Laporte from his front lawn while he was playing football with his family. Laporte had been a newspaper reporter before entering politics in 1961. He was now a prominent cabinet minister in the Bourassa Liberal government.

The day after his kidnapping, Laporte wrote the following letter to Premier Bourassa. He purposely misspelled several words to show that the FLQ was dictating the letter.

"My dear Robert, I feel like I am writing the most important letter I have ever written.

For the time being, I am in perfect health, and I am treated well, even courteously.

In short, the power to decide over my life is in your hands.

If there was only that involved, and the sacrifice of my life would bring good results, one could accept it....

You know how my personal situation deserves to draw attention. I had two brothers, both are now dead. I remain alone as the head of a large family that comprises my mother, my sisters, my own wife and my children, and the children of Rolland of whom I am the guardian. My departure would create for them irreparable grief, and you know the ties that bind the members of my family...

You have the power of life and death over me. I depend on you and I thank you for it.

Best regards,

Pierre Laporte"

THINK ABOUT YOUR ANSWERS TO THE FOLLOWING QUESTIONS, AND THEN WRITE PREMIER BOURASSA'S REPLY TO THE FLQ.

1. What does Laporte want Bourassa to do?
2. Since the FLQ asked Laporte to write this letter, and approved it, what influence do you think the FLQ had on its content?
3. Debate what you would you have done in Laporte's position.

Further Research

Books

To find out more about Canadian prime ministers, visit your local library. Most libraries have computers that connect to a database for researching information. If you input a key word, you will be provided with a list of books in the library that contain information on that topic. Non-fiction books are arranged numerically, using their call number. Fiction books are organized alphabetically by the author's last name.

Websites

The world wide web is also a good source of information. Reputable websites usually include government sites, educational sites, and online encyclopedias. Visit the following sites to learn more about Canadian prime ministers:

Click on "Prime Ministers Gallery" to watch CBC television and radio clips of interviews with Joe Clark and Pierre Trudeau.
http://archives.cbc.ca

In 2004, CBC had a contest for the Greatest Canadian. Pierre Trudeau was voted one of the top ten. To learn more visit CBC's website.
www.cbc.ca/greatest/top_ten

Read the obituary and eulogies that appeared shortly after Trudeau's death in 2000 in the *Globe and Mail*.
www.theglobeandmail.com/series/trudeau

Learn more about Joe Clark, John Turner, and other Canadian prime ministers by visiting Collections Canada's website.
www.collectionscanada.ca/primeministers

Glossary

anglophones: English-speaking people, especially in a country where there is more than one official language

apartheid: economic and political separation of Aboriginal Peoples from the rest of the population in South Africa

bilingualism: the ability to speak two languages

blacklisted: someone who is believed to deserve punishment, blame, or suspicion

Cold War: a period of diplomatic, economic, and psychological conflict between the United States and the former Soviet Union

conscripted: forced by the government to enlist in the armed forces

cruise missiles: guided self-contained precision bombs that are launched from ships or aircraft

denigrating: ruining a person's reputation

embargo: a restriction put on commerce by law

francophones: French-speaking people, especially in a country where there is more than one official language

greenhouse gases: gases in Earth's atmosphere that trap heat and warm Earth

manifesto: a public declaration of a person's or group of people's intentions

Métis: a person with both French and Aboriginal ancestry

Molotov cocktails: homemade bombs

multinational: a business organization with divisions in several nations

nationalism: pride in one's country

pacifist: a person who is strongly opposed to violence

patriating: bringing the Canadian government under the direct control of Canadians rather than British Parliament

Quiet Revolution: a period in Canadian history in which Francophone Quebeckers experienced a change in perspective regarding national identity

subsidizing: providing assistance with a grant of money

Political Terms

British North America Act: the British law that created the Dominion of Canada

cabinet minister: elected members of Parliament chosen by the prime minister to be responsible for specific areas, for example, health or Aboriginal affairs

civil service: people who work for the administration of the government

communist: a person that supports the political, social, and economic system in which the state owns all property, controls the production and distribution of goods and services, and controls the social and cultural life of the people

Confederation: the event in 1867 when Canada became its own country

Conservative Party: a party that does not support radical change

Constitution: the document which establishes the fundamental rules under which Canada is governed

federal government: the government of the country, as opposed to provincial or municipal governments

House of Commons: people who have been elected from across Canada to make laws for the whole country

leftist: a person who supports the equal distribution of rights, obligations, and wealth within the community

Liberal Party: a party supporting moderate change and reform

Marxist: a follower of Karl Marx's theories on communism

minority government: a government which holds half or fewer than half of the seats in the House of Commons

New Democratic Party (NDP): a party that supports government-funded social programs

non-confidence: the belief that a leader is no longer capable of leading, cumulating in a vote to remove that leader from power

North American Aerospace Defense Command (NORAD): a military alliance between Canada and the United States designed to defend North American air space

North Atlantic Treaty Organisation (NATO): military alliance of democratic states in Europe and North America

Parliament: the House of Commons and the Senate

Parti Québécois: a party supporting Quebec separatism

political activism: direct action in supporting one's own point of view on a political issue

premiers: Canadian provinces' heads of government

separatism: support of the withdrawal of a province from Confederation

Supreme Court: the highest court in Canada

Index